I0476040

Understanding What Leadership Means For IT Managers

Tips And Techniques That IT Managers Can Use In Order To Develop Leadership Skills

"Practical, proven techniques that will help you to manage your IT Manager career successfully"

Dr. Jim Anderson

Published by:
Blue Elephant Consulting
Tampa, Florida

Printed in the United States of America

Library of Congress Control Number: 2017903247

ISBN-13: 978-1544010557

ISBN-10: 1544010559

Warning – Disclaimer

The purpose of this book is to educate and entertain. This book
does not promise or guarantee that anyone following the ideas,
tips, suggestions, techniques or strategies will be successful. The
author, publisher and distributor(s) shall have neither liability
nor responsibility to anyone with respect to any loss or damage

caused, or alleged to be caused, directly or indirectly by the information contained in this book.

Recent Books By The Author

Product Management

- Manage Your Customers, Manage Your Product: Techniques For Product Managers To Better Understand What Their Customers Really Want

- Managing Your Product Manager Career: How Product Managers Can Find And Succeed In The Right Job

Public Speaking

- How To Get Ready To Give The Perfect Speech: What Tools To Use To Create Your Next Speech So That Your Message Will Be Remembered Forever!

- Creating Speeches That Work: How To Create A Speech That Will Make Your Message Be Remembered Forever!

CIO Skills

- How CIOs Can Take Their Career To The Next Level: How CIOs Can Work With The Entire Company In Order To Be Successful

- How CIOs Can Bring Business And IT Together: How CIOs Can Use Their Technical Skills To Help Their

Company Solve Real-World Business Problems

IT Manager Skills

- How IT Managers Can Use New Technology To Meet Today's IT Challenges: Technologies That IT Managers Can Use In Order to Make Their Teams More Productive

- How To Build High Performance IT Teams: Tips And Techniques That IT Managers Can Use In Order To Develop Productive Teams

Negotiating

- The Art Of Packaging A Negotiation: How To Develop The Skill Of Assembling Potential Trades In Order To Get The Best Possible Outcome

- Getting What You Want In A Negotiation By Learning How To Signal: How To Develop The Skill Of Effective Signaling In A Negotiation In Order To Get The Best Possible Outcome

Miscellaneous

- How To Heal A Broken Leg – Fast!: Understanding how to deal with a broken leg in order to start walking again quickly

- How Software Defined Networking (SDN) Is Going To Change Your World Forever: The Revolution In Network Design And How It Affects

Note: See a complete list of books by Dr. Jim Anderson at the back of this book.

Acknowledgements

Any book like this one is the result of years of real-world work experience. In my over 25 years of working for 7 different firms, I have met countless fantastic people and I've been mentored by some truly exceptional ones. Although I've probably forgotten some of the people who made me the person that I am today, here is my attempt to finally give them the recognition that they so truly deserve:

- Thomas P. Anderson
- Art Puett
- Bobbi Marshall
- Bob Boggs

Dr. Jim Anderson

This book is dedicated to my wife Lori. None of this would have been possible without her love and support.

Thanks for the best years of my life (so far)...!

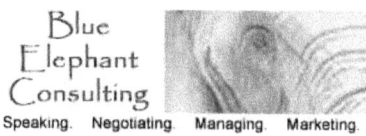

Speaking.   Negotiating.   Managing.   Marketing.

Table Of Contents

To Be A Leader, You Have To Understand What Leadership Is

Leadership is one of those things that we all think that we know what it is, but we are hard pressed to describe it to someone if they ask us. This makes picking the next generation of leaders that much harder. We want them to have the leadership skills that we know that they need, but how can we make sure that they have them? Some IT manager revert to using the time-tested trial-by-fire approach, but is this really the best way?

When we think about leaders, we envision them out in front of the team encouraging everyone onward. However, in real life it often doesn't happen this way. Sure, we may have the title of a leader, but what should we do if we have not been given the responsibility? Additionally, does a leader always have to be out in front? It just might be possible to lead from behind.

We're not always placed in charge of the team that our career may depend on. When this happens, we need to find ways to lead the team despite not having the official responsibility to do so. In these cases, we'll be considered by the team to be part of the team and this makes our leadership challenge that much more difficult as we attempt to lead the team from inside.

Every time that we are placed in a leadership position, our success is not guaranteed. There will always be risk associated with what we are trying to do. This means that it's going to be up to us to find a way to both manage and deal with that risk. We are also going to have to be aware that we won't always be successful. We will occasionally fail and when this happens, we need to have a plan to deal with it.

In any firm we may not have much of a say on who is on our team. However, when nepotism comes into play, things can become a lot trickier for an IT manager. We'll have to find a way to deal with this while at the same time trying to uncover ways that we can motivate our entire team.

To show leadership to your team, you need to be able to communicate with them. There are many different ways to go about doing this, but more often than not, giving an effective speech is the most direct. This is a skill that every IT manager has to work at. Public speaking is a tool that will permit you to show your leadership skills.

For more information on what it takes to be a great IT manager, check out my blog, The Accidental IT Leader, at:

www.TheAccidentalITLeader.com

Good luck!

-    Dr. Jim Anderson

About The Author

I must confess that I never set out to be a CIO. When I went to school, I studied Computer Science and thought that I'd get a nice job programming and that would be that. Well, at least part of that plan worked out!

My first job was working for Boeing on their F/A-18 fighter jet program. I spent my days programming fighter jet software in assembly language and I loved it. The U.S. government decided to save some money and went looking for other countries to sell this plane to. This put me into an unfamiliar role: I started to meet with foreign military officials and I ended up having to manage groups of engineers who were working on international projects.

Time moved on and so did I. I found myself working for Siemens, the big German telecommunications company. They were making phone switches and selling them to the seven U.S. phone companies. The problem was that the switches were too complicated. Customers couldn't tell the difference between one complicated phone switch from another complicated phone switch. Once again I found myself working with the sales and marketing teams to find ways to make the great technology that the engineers had developed understandable to both internal and external customers.

I've spent over 25 years working as a senior IT professional for both big companies and startups. This has given me an opportunity to learn what it takes to manage and IT department in ways that allow it to maximize its output while becoming a valuable part of the overall company.

I now live in Tampa Florida where I spend my time managing my consulting business, Blue Elephant Consulting, teaching college courses at the University of South Florida, and traveling to work with companies like yours to share the knowledge that I have about how to create and manage successful IT departments.

I'm always available to answer questions and I can be reached at:

Dr. Jim Anderson
Blue Elephant Consulting
Email: jim@BlueElephantConsulting.com
Facebook: http://goo.gl/1TVoK
Web: **www.BlueElephantConsulting.com**

"Unforgettable communication skills that will set your ideas free..."

Create IT Departments That Are Productive And A Valuable Asset To The Rest Of The Company !

Dr. Jim Anderson is available to provide training and coaching on the topics that are the most important to people who have to manage IT departments: how can I build a productive IT department (and keep it together) while at the same time providing the rest of the company with the IT services that they need?

Dr. Anderson believes that in order to both learn and remember what he says, speakers need to laugh. Each one of his speeches is full of fun and humor so that what he says "sticks" with everyone.

Dr. Anderson's CIO Skills Training Includes:

1. How to identify and attract the right type of IT workers to your IT department.
2. How to build relationships with the company's senior management in order to get the support that you need?
3. How to stay on top of changing technology and security issues so that you never get surprised?

Dr. Jim Anderson works with over 100 customers per year. To invite Dr. Anderson to work with you, contact him at:

Phone: 813-418-6970 or
Email: jim@BlueElephantConsulting.com

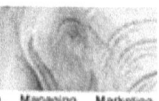

Blue Elephant Consulting

Speaking. Negotiating. Managing. Marketing.

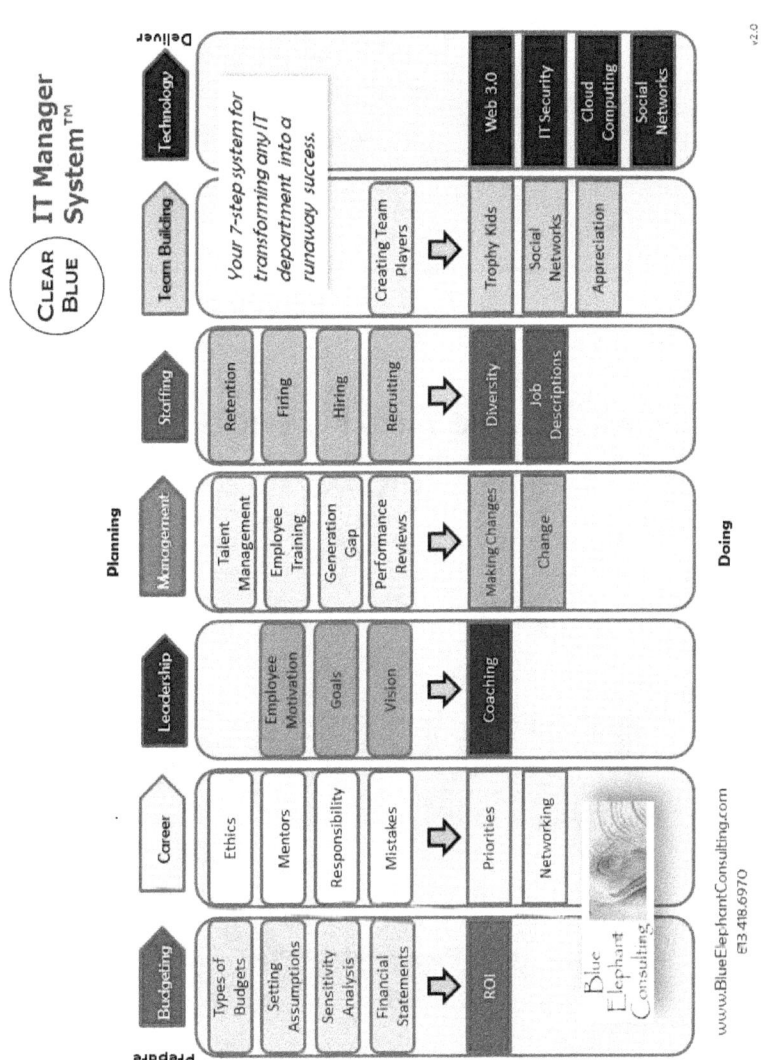

The **Clear Blue IT Manager System™** has been created to provide IT managers with a clear roadmap for how to manage an IT team. This system shows IT Managers what needs to be done and in what order to do it.

Chapter 1

You Can Be An IT Leader, Here's How...

Chapter 1: You Can Be An IT Leader, Here's How...

Congratulations, you are finally an IT manager. Does that mean that you are also **an IT leader**? Turns out that the answer to that question is no. So what's the difference? Employees do what a manager tells them to do because they have to. Employees do what a leader tells them to do because they want to. Clearly we all need to find out what we need to do in order to become leaders...

What Do IT Leaders Do?

Aren't an IT manager and an IT leader really just two different words for the same person? No, they are not. A manager is able to work with a team in order to create a kind of order out of the normal chaos of life. A leader, on the other hand, is able to deal with **ambiguity, change, and opportunity** all at the same time.

Although we often associate leaders with that touchy-feely big vision stuff, it can be easy to overlook one important point. **Leaders know how to get results**. What's even more impressive is that IT leaders are able to get these results by convincing not only the people who work for them, but also large parts of the rest of the company to subscribe to their vision and work with them to make their vision a reality.

To become a leader, you need to always be aware. **Leaders move fast**. They have the ability to recognize both threats and opportunities when they see them. They use their positive energy and they pull together a response that is able to meet the challenges that they encounter.

How Do IT Leaders Do It?

Everyone wants to be an IT leader, but **very few ever make it**. One reason for this is because many people don't fully understand what it takes to be a leader.

Some people are born with many of the leader traits that are needed in order to be successful. However, the rest of us have to **find leader role models**, watch them closely and understand what set of traits we need to develop further.

IT leaders have **a set of characteristics** that allow them to fill the role of leader. These characteristics include being caring, being comfortable with not having all of the facts, being persistent, and being a good communicator. These are the skills that you can learn how to develop by finding leaders who are good at them and observing them closely.

What All Of This Means For You

As an IT manager, your ultimate goal should be **to become an IT leader**. Employees will follow and do what a leader tells them to do because they believe in the vision that the leader has laid out for them.

IT leaders get things done – **they produce real results**. However, they are able to do this by getting people who don't work for them to complete work for them simply because they believe in what the leader is trying to accomplish. IT leaders are able to make this happen because of their personal characteristics that include being caring, persistent, and good communicators.

Every IT manager can become an IT leader. What it requires is for you to locate **a good IT leader that you can emulate**. By observing closely and developing leadership skills, you can become the person who can accomplish anything.

Chapter 2

IT Managers Know That Trial By Fire Is The Best Way To Pick New IT Leaders

Chapter 2: IT Managers Know That Trial By Fire Is The Best Way To Pick New IT Leaders

I've got some bad news for all of you IT Managers out there: it turns out that 25% of the best workers in your IT team are planning on leaving within the next 12 months. Not to depress you even more, but it turns out that those internal job change programs that you have perhaps created that are intended to develop the next generation of IT leaders don't seem to be working – 40% of the internal rotations that are made by IT "high-pots" (high potential) employees end up in failure. Let's take a look at **what problems you need to solve ...**

Problem: The Wrong People Are Managing Your Top Talent

Jean Martin and Conrad Schmidt are researchers who have been looking into **what makes leadership transitions successful**. What they have discovered is basically bad news for IT managers.

In order for an IT manager to grow their star talent, managers need to be able to first identify who this talent is and then they need to find ways to put them in positions of increasing responsibility in order to get them ready to lead the company. All too often this isn't happening.

The people in the IT department who are best able to **initially identify high potential candidates** are the coworkers who are working with these IT workers. If developing the best and the brightest talent is left to these members of the IT department, it's just not going to happen.

Instead, what needs to happen is that you as an IT manager need to **actively participate in the process**. This means that you need to work with the rest of your team so that when potential star talent is identified, they can be slotted into development programs. Make sure that you reward coworkers for finding high-quality talent so that they'll be motivated to share their best with you and won't be tempted to hoard those workers that they believe can make their lives easier.

Problem: Playing Over-Protective Parent To Your Up-And-Coming Future IT Leaders

Once you've identified your star IT talent and you've got them enrolled in your talent development program, you really don't want them to fail. **Or do you?**

All too often what IT managers do is to hand pick the assignments that are given to up-and-coming IT managers. The goal is to find positions where they will be challenged, **but not too much**. Since you've already invested time and energy in getting them this far (and since there are a limited number of stars), you really don't want them to fall flat on their face. This means that you don't want to place them in a position where they might fail.

This is the wrong thinking. Although yes, you really don't want to put anyone in a situation where they can't win, at the same time you do want to put your best performers in difficult situations so that they can have a chance to become **"battle hardened"**. The military does this all the time – you have to have seen actual combat if you want to eventually become a General someday.

Only by coming face-to-face with a truly difficult IT / business situation will your talent be able to **prove their mettle**. Yes, some will fold under the pressure, but you'd rather find it out now than later on when you've invested even more in them. Place your best talent in situations where they can prove that they really are the best that your IT team has to offer.

What All Of This Means For You

Nobody ever said that growing the next round of IT leaders was going to be easy, but who knew that it was going to be this tough? Ensuring that the firm has a deep bench of future talent is one of an IT manager's **key jobs**.

Mistakes that an IT manager needs to avoid when developing talent include allowing top talent to be **discovered and managed by coworkers**. These individuals are too important to be left to chance within the small world of a given team. The other mistake is for IT managers to work too hard to shield their star talent from failures. Talent needs to be exposed to challenging circumstances in order to be given the ability to fully develop.

IT managers need to understand that they can't put their best and brightest staff in a closet with the hopes that they can bring them out when the need arises. Instead, they need to **spend time every day** working to ensure that the talent is growing and getting ready for the positions that they'll eventually fill.

Chapter 3

You're Not In Charge IT Manager – Now Lead!

Chapter 3: You're Not In Charge IT Manager

Talk about whining! I can't tell you how many times I've been working with newly minted IT managers who come to me and complain that people aren't listening to what they say. A little bit of digging on my part and I discover that they're part of some sort of **cross functional team** or that they are working with vendors. They've found themselves in the classic situation where they need to lead a group of people who don't report to them. Good luck!

All The Responsibility, None Of The Authority

How many times have we all found ourselves in this situation? Our management has tasked us with solving some problem and put us on a team that we are supposed to lead. Unfortunately, they forgot to tell anyone that **we're in charge!**

IT managers can generally get things done by telling people who work for them what they need to be doing. Clearly this strategy won't work when you are a member of a team of people who don't work for you. All too often I find the IT managers that I'm coaching struggle to **switch gears** – they keep trying to tell people what they need to be doing. They then become frustrated when their directives go unnoticed.

Let us agree on one thing: when you are not in charge, you can't just **"take over" by brute force**. That's never going to work. Instead, you are going to need to find a way to get the rest of the team to "elect" you to be their leader.

That Leadership Thing

In the end, this all boils down to a question of leadership. When you are a part of a team and **nobody directly reports to you**, you're going to have to lead them, not manage them.

You really can't ask the rest of the team to **accept you as their leader**, you need to show them that they should accept you. This is not a formal thing – no vote will be taken. It will be your attitudes, attributes, and your behavior that will make them accept you. If you can convince them to accept you as their leader, then it will just happen.

Finally, what are **the criteria** that will make the rest of the team accept you as their leader? It comes down to several things. Your reputation will be an important part of their decision – are you known for performing hard work? Are you honest? Do you have the ability to bring good ideas to the table? Your ability to be accepted as a leader will be based on how others perceive you on these topics.

What All Of This Means For You

IT leaders often find themselves in situations where they are expected to lead a team that **does not report to them**. At first this can be an overwhelming situation – how ever are they going to get anything accomplished?

The secret to getting a team to accomplish a shared goal, no matter if the members of the team report to you or not, is to **show them leadership**. Your ability to convey a clear sense of purpose, the ability to be relied on, and a demonstration of subject matter expertise will convince the team to follow your direction.

Although what needs to be done may be clear, by no means is this an easy task to accomplish. As I tell the IT managers that I'm working with, if leadership was easy, then you'd see everyone doing it. As you struggle to do this task correctly, take comfort in the realization that the skill that you are developing is exactly the skill that you'll need **when you get promoted!**

Chapter 4

Leading From Behind: Learn & Engage

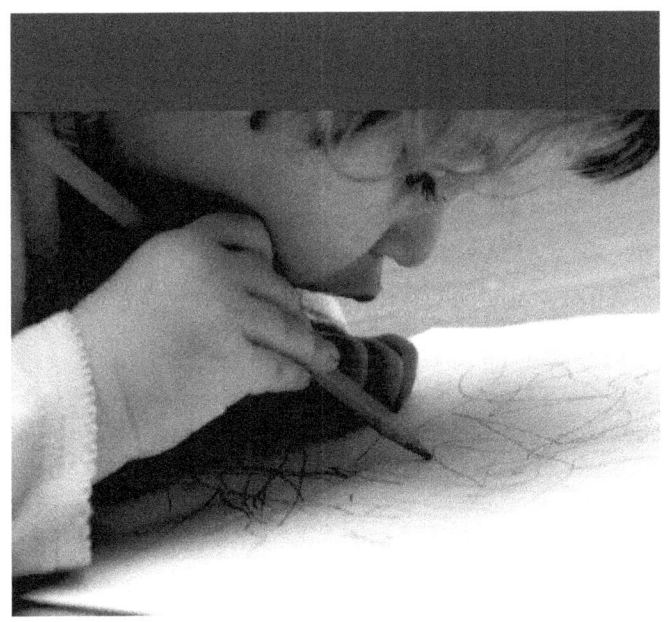

Chapter 4: Leading From Behind: Learn & Engage

When I work with IT Leaders who are looking for ways to get that next promotion, I tell them that they are going to need to demonstrate leadership. This is an easy thing for me to say and a very hard thing for them to do. Complicating matters even more is the fact that IT managers are finding themselves drafted onto teams that they are just members of, **not leaders of**. What's an IT manager to do?

Learn Early, Learn Often

As IT managers, we all realize that we certainly **don't know it all**. However, when we find ourselves part of a team that we are not leading, it can become frustrating when we realize just how much the team doesn't know.

The classic solution to this type of problem is to have the team stumble forward and complete the project that they have been assigned to work on. When the project is over, upper management steps in and **an after-action review** is conducted in order to provide everyone with an understanding of what went well and what could have been done better.

That's all fine and good, but if you want to use your skills to manage the situation even better, you can make a suggestion. Instead of waiting until the project is over, suggest that the team **conduct so called "mini reviews"** on an ongoing basis. Depending on how fast the team is moving, these reviews could be done once a day or more likely once a week.

Getting the team to take the time to step back and understand how things are going even as the project is underway is a great way to **keep things on track**. Even though you aren't managing the team, it's suggestions like this that can allow the team to benefit from your management skills.

Engage With Others

Think back to the last team that you were a member of. Did everyone else on that team **contribute equally to the success of the project?** I suspect that the answer is no.

Once again, even if you have not been asked to manage the team, you can still **contribute to making the team a success**. Every person on the team has their own set of skills and talents. Likewise there are a diverse set of tasks that the team needs to accomplish.

Matching the right people to the right tasks is a key part of what IT managers do. While you are part of a team, you can take the initiative and **create two lists**: who is on the team and what skills they bring to the table and a list of what tasks need to be accomplished. By matching the people with the tasks, you will ensure that everyone gets involved in working towards the team's ultimate goals. The trick here will be to get the team to agree to having the individuals perform the tasks – you can make suggestions, but you can't make anyone to do anything.

What All Of This Means For You

When IT managers find themselves working as part of a team and not leading the team, **it can be a confusing situation**. What they need to realize is that management is not something that can be handed to them, in this situation they need to earn it.

One way to help the team to manage itself is to create situations where the team will be able to **dynamically learn even as it is doing**. This can be done by setting up weekly or even daily reviews of what the team has accomplished, where it has run into problems, and what needs to be changed.

Another issue that the team may encounter is that **not all of its members are being fully utilized**. Taking the time to do the extra work that is required to match team member's skills to tasks that need to be done allows everyone to be engaged and to contribute.

IT managers who have not been asked to manage a team that they are part of can still **lend their management skills** to ensuring that the team will be successful. Consider this to be good training for when you are promoted into senior IT management positions!

Chapter 5

Turns Out That The Secret To Leading A Team From The Inside Is...

Chapter 5: Turns Out That The Secret To Leading A Team From The Inside Is...

When I work with IT Leaders who are looking for ways to get that next promotion, I tell them that they are going to need to demonstrate leadership. This is an easy thing for me to say and a very hard thing for them to do. Complicating matters even more is the fact that IT managers are finding themselves drafted onto teams that they are just members of, **not leaders of**. What's an IT manager to do?

The Secret Of Feedback

Here in the 21st Century you'd think that IT managers would have all of the tools available to them that they would need **in order to be successful** even when they are working as part of a larger team. And although this is true, if you really want to be successful you're going to need to learn to use the most important tool of all: feedback.

So just what is this thing that we call feedback? Sure we all think that we know what it is, but do we really? Often times the IT managers that I'm working with view feedback as **simply remembering to talk with their team members** every so often.

Feedback is so much more than that. The key is that feedback, when done correctly, is not something that you do **casually or "off the cuff"**. At the same time feedback does not need to be done in a formal environment (although it can be).

Feedback is how you as a manager can provide other members of a team that you are working on with **a reflection of how they are doing** even if they don't work for you. This is critical feedback because you may be the only person who can provide them with an accurate view of their job performance.

When done correctly feedback provides a mix of both **encouragement and correction to your staff**. You need to take the time to do things as simple as providing your fellow team members with encouragement (""Hey, great job on that report.") as well as suggestions for doing a better job ("Maybe next time you can tone down your voice a bit when you are presenting…").

How To Use Feedback Correctly

Feedback is a fantastic tool for IT managers to use. It's free, easy to use, and we are all born with the ability to do it. To manage the team that you are working on effectively, you need to learn to use this tool in a way that will allow you to **get the most out of your team**.

One of the most effective ways to use feedback that I've found is as a way to provide **a gentle guiding hand** to team members who may be in the process of making a poor decision. As we all know, providing guidance to team members is one of a manager's most important tasks (and one of the hardest to do).

The way that I use feedback to accomplish this is to **share stories of past accomplishments**. When a member of a team is facing a new challenge, a good idea is to have the manager sit down with the team member and use feedback to have a conversation with them about what the best way to proceed is. Saying something along the lines of "You know, I faced a similar situation like this a while ago and what I did to solve it was…" This kind of feedback can provide the gentle nudge that is needed to keep your team members on track…

What All Of This Means For You

In the never ending quest to become better IT managers, we are all looking for ways to **use our skills to manage our teams**. New management fads come and go, however the ones that work are always available for us to use.

One technique that IT managers have used over and over again, is the **feedback technique**. You need to take the time to have a real conversation with your team members and use the feedback session to really connect with them. Additionally, you can use feedback to help team members make decisions based on situations that you've faced in the past.

Being an IT manager has never been an easy job. However, having the feedback technique to use makes your ability to **connect with your team** and keep them on the right path that much easier.

Chapter 6

IT Manager Leadership: Two Ways To Lead When You're Not In Charge

Chapter 6: IT Manager Leadership: Two Ways To Lead When You're Not In Charge

When I work with IT Leaders who are looking for ways to get that next promotion, I tell them that they are going to need to demonstrate leadership. This is an easy thing for me to say and a very hard thing for them to do. Complicating matters even more is the fact that IT managers are finding themselves drafted onto teams that they are just members of, **not leaders of**. What's an IT manager to do?

It's Always All About Goals

When an IT manager is told to work as part of a team but not told to manage it, it can be easy to treat this as **a low priority task** if you aren't appointed to run the show. I mean really, you've got other tasks that you are responsible for and you're running the show there.

However, that would be a mistake on your part. It turns out that in real life senior management are often put on teams that they may not have been told to manage. If you can demonstrate the ability to work with and to even lead this type of team, you'll be demonstrating skills that will **make you a candidate for a promotion**.

The first thing that you need to do when you become part of a team that you are not leading is to encourage the team to take the time to write down what they are hoping to achieve. Step up and lead the discussion as the team tries to clarify what their **shared objectives** are.

To Get The Right Answers, You Need To Know How To Think Correctly

Teams can be **a confusing mess**. There are all sorts of people and everybody thinks that they know how to solve the problem that the team has been asked to take care of. More often than not the first team meeting dissolves into a set of isolated conversations and not much gets accomplished.

You have an opportunity to **show leadership** in this situation. You can help the team actually accomplish something by showing them how to apply systematic thinking to the problem at hand.

Instead of just randomly breaking off pieces of the problem and then attempting to do a deep dive and come up with a solution for it, instead **take a step back**. Start by making sure that all of the needed data has been gathered.

Next take the time to determine how the current situation was created. Once you get group agreement on that move on and identify **a set of possible solutions**. It's going to be much easier to get the team to select a workable solution from a set of possible solutions instead of trying to build solutions from the ground up with only various parts of the required data.

What Does All Of This Mean For You

IT managers will always be finding themselves in situations where they have not explicitly been put in charge of providing management to a team. When this happens to you, there are two ways that you can deal with it: give up and complain about the situation or **choose to demonstrate your leadership skills**.

In order to show leadership and how you can manage a team, you need to start by **creating a set of clear objectives** that the group can work towards – goals if you like. This will provide direction for the team. Next, show the team how to think in a systematic fashion. Lay out the challenges, identify the constraints, and then start to identify solutions.

Leadership is a tricky thing. It's not something that is handed to you, rather **you have to earn it**. IT managers who master the ability to create goals that a team will accept and then show the team how to think systematically will be one step closer to earning the leadership of that team.

Chapter 7

---

5 Things That An IT Manager Needs To Know About Risk

Chapter 7: 5 Things That An IT Manager Needs To Know About Risk

How much time every day do you spend thinking about risk? No matter what your answer was, I'm willing to bet that **you are not spending enough time** on this important subject. Every IT manager knows that there are risks all around us each and every day. In fact, the number of risks that your IT team is facing is probably growing every day. The big question that you need to have the IT manager skills to answer is what should you be doing about this?

5 Things That An IT Manager Needs To Know About Risk Management

When starting to think about how you want to deal with all of the risks that your IT team is facing, **things can become overwhelming very quickly** because none of us have had IT manager training that taught us how to deal with this issue. What you need to do is to take the time to prioritize how you are going to be spending your time. Here are 5 things that you are going to have to know about how to most effectively tackle your risk issues:

Start With What You Know: Of course every IT manager should start out by making sure that the key risk areas that their IT team is facing are covered. Key areas to be covered include making sure that your team won't experience any data breaches. Once you've got this all taken care of, it's time to look beyond the just your team and take a look at the entire IT department. Take the time to understand how the IT department is using all of that data that is gathered and see if other IT teams are exposing themselves to risk as they use what you've given them.

Don't Get Caught Up In Compliance: It can be all too easy for an IT manager to become focused on a given compliance project (HIPPA, Sarbanes-Oxley, etc.) and be left with the false sense that they've got their risk under control. These programs can help you manage your risk, but they don't do it all. What you want to do is to stay ahead of the risks that your company is going to be facing and if you are just spending your time trying to be compliant, then you're going to end up falling behind.

Look On The Bright Side: With all of the other projects that an IT manager has on his or her plate, risk management may not be the one that you really want to spend much of your time working on. However, you need to realize that this type of program will provide you with an opportunity to learn more about the IT department's overall business processes and how it uses its data. Having a good understanding of this should only help to further your career.

It's All Been Done Before: The good news about setting up a risk management program for your IT team is that you are not the first IT manager to do this. It turns out that there are a number of different "cheat sheets" that you can use to get your program off of the ground. These include ISO 31000, and ISACA's Risk-IT. However, as with all such templates, you need to keep in mind that these were not created with an understanding of your particular IT team's needs. You're going to have to take the time to find out how to modify them to fit the way that your company operates.

Know Who You Are Up Against: Every risk program has to be started by having you sit down and spend some time thinking about just exactly who you are trying to protect your team from. Yes, there are the usual list of external suspects. The hackers and others who are trying to get their hands on your team's most valuable secrets via social engineering or other methods. However, you also have to keep in mind that your greatest threats may be coming from other members of your company. These are the ones who are already on the inside and who may be able to do the most harm in the least amount of time.

What All Of This Means For You

IT managers may think that they have a more important job to do besides risk management for their IT team (such as IT team building), but I wouldn't know what it would be. One of the biggest challenges that IT managers face when trying to create a risk management program is that **it can be confusing as to just exactly where they should start**.

In order to get your risk management efforts off to a good start, **there are 5 things that you need to do**. You need to start the program by securing your IT team and then following the data into other IT teams and making sure that they are secure also. Realize that compliance programs are good, but they are not enough. View creating a compliance program as a true career opportunity for you. Everything has been done before and that means that you can use "cheat sheets" to get your program started. Finally, make sure that you understand who you are up against so that you can create the right type of program.

Although most IT managers would rather spend their time working on programs that have to do with mobility or cloud computing, it's the risk management program that they create **that may be of the most value to their company**. Take the time to understand what you want to do and how you're going to do it and you'll be able to create a program that will keep your IT team's intellectual property safe and secure.

Chapter 8

IT Managers Want To Know: What Makes IT Teams Fail?

Chapter 8: IT Managers Want To Know: What Makes IT Teams Fail?

As an IT manager you are hoping you can use your IT manager skills in order to ensure that your team will be successful. That they'll be able to complete the work assignments that you are given on time, under budget, and at a high quality. That's a great goal; however, **why is it that all too often IT teams fail?** It turns out that there are 3 main reasons that an IT team can fail and you had better know what they are if you want to avoid making these mistakes.

Misalignment

One of the most glaring problems that IT managers run into is that **their teams are working on the wrong problems.** The company's leaders know that they are facing a set of challenges that they need the IT department to help them solve. However, somehow in the communication of those problems to IT something gets mixed up. Making sure that we're working on the right project was never a part of our IT manager training.

The end result of this is that you and your team set off working on a project that even if you complete it successfully **will not result in any tangible benefit for the company.** You are not going to be able to help them find solutions to the real challenges that they are facing.

A common term for this type of disconnect is "being out of alignment". Everyone realizes that it is a real problem, it's just that nobody seems to have a good solution for solving it. Ultimately, it's going to be up to you to find a way **to make sure that your team is working on the right projects.**

Death Of A Project

If you do any searching online about the failure rate of IT projects, you are going to discover that up to 80% of IT projects end in failure. That is an enormous number. In fact, it's so high that the rest of the company has started to adopt an attitude that just because you start an IT project **does not mean that you are going to be able to deliver what you are promising**.

When an IT project fails, **the failure hurts the reputation of both you and your IT team**. The part of the business that was counting on you creating a solution to their problem is left just a bit poorer for the experience and they still have the problem that they had originally.

As an IT manager you need to be aware that the chances of your next IT project failing are great. This means that you need to keep your eyes open and be **looking for the tell-tale signs of a project starting to fail** and take action to save the project when you see these.

Communication Failure

As an IT manager, we often ask ourselves what **the #1 skill that we need to have is**. We can get caught up in the hot topic of the day (cloud computing, big data, etc.) and think that one of our technical skills is what makes us a good manager. However, we'd be wrong. It turns out that our success as an IT manager rests on our ability to communicate clearly.

The ability to communicate what we want to other people is critical for several reasons. As an IT manager, **we need to get things done**. We need a wide range of people to do what we need them to do when we need them to do it. The only way that this is going to happen is if we are able to make them clearly understand what we want them to do and why it needs to be done. When it comes to IT team building, your communication skills are what is going to make it happen.

Communication is not just restricted to the members of our IT team. We also have to be able to **clearly communicate with the outside world** that consists of other people in the company and even potentially customers. We'll need different vocabularies and different ways of both talking and listening in order to get the most out of each of these communication opportunities.

What All Of This Means For You

Being an IT manager is not an easy job. You are trying to get difficult to manage talented people to use cutting edge technology in order to solve real-word business problems. **Your success is not guaranteed** and in fact if you are not aware of the three biggest pitfalls that you and your team may encounter, you could be headed for disaster.

An IT team **exists to do the work that is needed by the rest of the business**. If the work that you are doing is not the work that they need to have done, you've got a real problem. IT projects are difficult to complete on time and under budget. In fact they often fail to deliver what the company expected and so you've got some serious management to do if you want your team's project to have a chance of succeeding. Finally, forget the technical skills that you need to have – the ability to communicate both inside and outside of your team is going to be what determines your long term success.

I don't mean to be all doom and gloom – **it is possible to be a successful IT manager**. However, you need to go into this with your eye wide open and realize that it's all too easy to lead your team down the wrong path. Be aware of the easy ways to go wrong and you'll be able to do a better job of avoiding them!

Chapter 9

How IT Managers Deal With The "N" Word – "Nepotism"

Chapter 9: How IT Managers Deal With The "N" Word – "Nepotism"

Just exactly how did you get your IT manager job? Did you get it because you worked hard and you showed the powers that be that you had IT manager skills and just how good of a leader you could be so that they promoted you? Or did you get promoted because of who you know – dad, mom, grandpa, etc? If you got your IT manager job for all the wrong reasons, then your life is going to become a lot harder in the future...

What is Nepotism & Why Is It Bad?

When an IT worker gets promoted to be a manager and is placed in charge of a team, they have been given authority by the company, but not by the team. In order to get authority from the team, **you need to earn it** and no amount of IT manager training is going to make this happen. If you've gotten your IT manager job by having a special relationship with the boss or because you are related to somebody important (nepotism), you now have a bit of a mess on your hands.

Getting the manager job means that on paper you have the authority to do the tasks that will be required of you. However, your ability to accomplish those tasks is going to rest on **your team doing the work** and if they don't view you as having the responsibility to tell them what to do, you've got a problem on your hands.

If you find yourself in this unenviable situation where your team believes that you've gotten a job that you may not have deserved, then you're going to have to **take the time to prove yourself to them**. You are going to need to get beyond the lip-service that your team will be giving you and find ways to truly earn their respect.

How Should IT Managers Be Selected?

If nepotism is not the right way to select IT managers, what then is the correct method? One key point that all too many companies don't realize is that good technical skills don't necessarily mean that someone is going to make a good IT manager. All too often engineers who have been big contributors to a project **get promoted based on the quality of work that they delivered**. This is just wrong, wrong, wrong.

Instead, what should be used to determine who should be promoted to be an IT manager is **that something special inside of them**. Call it what you want, perhaps a "spark of leadership", but it's that hard-to-define personal characteristic that shows that you'd make a good leader.

Good IT managers are able to provide their teams with **sound leadership**. Their sense of judgment is respected by their team and people value their opinions. An IT manager needs to have the self-confidence to make the tough decisions when the situation calls for it.

What Is A Real IT Leader?

Which gets us to the ultimate question: **what is a real IT leader?** If you are going to want to be an effective leader of an IT team, then you are going to have to win the respect of your team. I'd hope that you got the job because you deserved it, but no matter how you got there, you need to show your team that they should follow you.

True IT leaders have the ability to **accurately see into the future**. You can't just make decisions in a vacuum. Instead, you need to be able to understand how any decision that you make today is going to change the future tomorrow.

Managing people is never an easy task. People are messy creatures that come with all sorts of baggage. However, an effective IT leader has the ability to **focus on the facts when making a decision**. Yes, the human factor is important, but your decisions have to rise above the people involved while not forgetting that the decision will ultimately impact them.

What All Of This Means For You

When you become an IT manager, you want to have the respect and support of the team that you will be managing. Getting the job **because of who you know** or because of what family you were born into is NOT the right way to become an IT manager.

If you are related to the boss, then **you're going to have a hard road ahead of you**. Winning the respect of your team is going to be a challenge no matter how much IT team building you do because they are all going to assume that you didn't earn the job that you got. The right way to select an IT manager is to be recognized for your leadership skills. Real IT managers have the ability to see the future and guide their teams towards it.

You will only be a successful IT manager **with the support of your team**. Take the time to work with them and convince them that you have your position because you are the right person for the job. If you can do this, then all of sudden your job as an IT manager just got a lot easier.

Chapter 10

How An IT Leader Can Motivate Their Team

Chapter 10: How An IT Leader Can Motivate Their Team

Having an IT team report to you is a great complement – the company believes that you can lead them to success. However, in order to get your team to accomplish the things that you want them to do, you are going to have to first motivate them to take action. This motivation thing can be tricky, **who among us really knows how to go about doing it?** Looks like this is one more of the IT manager skills that we all need to master.

Just Exactly What Do You Want Your Team To Do?

Before you can motivate your team to accomplish great things, you are first going to have to make sure that you understand what you want them to do. The one thing that you are going to want to avoid doing is presenting them with **confusing or contradictory messages**. Knowing how to do this is something that we really should have all received IT manager training on. Assuming that that has not happened, perhaps we'll need to do something about it...

One thing that will be very important for you to realize is how they may view what you are asking them to accomplish. Often times, your request may come across as **being irrational**. Often when we want our teams to accomplish great things, what we are asking them to do will appear to be impossible at first.

Just because it can be very difficult to motivate your IT team does not mean that it shouldn't be done. Instead, that means that **it is that much more important**. The company has things that it desperately needs to have accomplished and it is looking to your team in order to find a way to get these things done.

How To Motivate A Team

Knowing that you want to motivate a team and **knowing how to motivate a team** are two completely different things. One thing that you need to do right off the bat is to make sure that your team knows that you don't view them as one big team. Rather, you are going to have to show them that you view them as being individuals.

Next, you are going to have to convince them that **you trust them to complete the role that they are being asked to play**. This trust is a key part of getting them to commit to accomplishing what you are asking them to do. Finally, you need to make sure that they understand that what they are doing is important and that it matters to the company's ability to accomplish a higher cause.

Just getting your team pumped up to take on a big challenge is not going to be enough. If you leave it at this, then they may very quickly start to forget why they agreed to follow you. Instead, once they are motivated and working towards accomplishing the shared goal, you need to spend your time **being out there with the team while they are working**. It is only by working side-by-side with them that you'll be able to show them that you support what they are doing.

What This Means For You

As an IT leader, one of the tasks that you are going to be expected to do is to **motivate your team**. Think of this as a form of IT team building. That means that you are going to have to be able to convince them to perform an IT task no matter how big or challenging it may seem.

Before you can motivate your team, you first have to make sure that you **know what you want them to do for you**. You need to understand that what you may be asking them to do is either hard or even impossible. In order to motivate them you are going to have to show them that you care about them as individuals. You will also have to show them that you trust them to accomplish the tasks that you are entrusting them with.

Motivation is a skill that can be learned. We need to study the people around us and understand who already has this skill. By studying how they do it, we can grow our own motivational talent. If you can get good at motivating your team, then they will be able to go on and accomplish great things!

Chapter 11

How To Deliver A Great Speech To Your Team

Chapter 11: How To Deliver A Great Speech To Your Team

How big is your IT team? If you are a successful IT manager, your company will recognize that you have great IT manager skills and they will keep assigning more and more people to your team. What this means for you is that very quickly it is going to get hard to **get your message out to the entire team**. Yes, you can send an email blast, but that lacks the human element. A much better skill to have is the ability to deliver a speech to your team.

It's Your Story

If you are like most of us, this speaking in public thing is **not something that you feel very comfortable doing**. Sorry, most IT manager training doesn't cover this. When a situation arises in which you are going to have to stand up in front of your team, one of the first things that will cross your mind is "how am I going to pull this off?"

All too often the answer that we come up with is to try to emulate someone else. Undoubtedly there is someone at your company who actually does a good job of talking to a crowd. You've probably seen them present a 100 times and so you think that **if you just copy their style then you'll do all right**.

Well, it turns out that that approach generally does not work. Instead, you end up leaving your audience with the feeling that you were not genuine. What you tell them will come out sounding contrived and they'll miss the point of what you were trying to tell them. Instead, a much better approach is to take the time to **map out the structure of your talk**. Come up with a flow for your message that best matches your personal style.

Know Your Audience

One of the scariest things that any of us will ever have to do in this life is to stand in front of a bunch of people **that we don't know** and give a talk. You need to take steps to make sure that you never find yourself in this position.

What this means for you is that before the time arrives for you to start to give your speech you've got some work to do. You are going to want to take the time to **meet your audience**. Mix with them and have a lot of small talk with them. Your goal is to introduce yourself and to find out more about them.

The goal of introducing yourself to your audience long before you start to speak is twofold. Your first goal is to **get to know your audience**. What are their cares and concerns? Knowing this you can adjust your speech accordingly. Secondly, when you start to deliver your speech it sure would be nice if there were some friendly faces in the crowd. Suddenly giving that speech won't be so scary.

Turns Out That It's Not All About You

All too often when we determine that giving a speech is what we have to do, **we get all caught up in the message**. We start to think to ourselves that the reason that we're giving the speech is to deliver the message and the audience should be grateful that we're taking the time to do it.

It turns out that this is the wrong approach. Instead what we should be thinking is that **we've got some great information** and how cool would it be to share it with our audience.

If you can approach your speech in this manner, then it will seem to you more like you are providing your audience with **a type of service that they want**. When you can do this, it will transform what used to be a speech into something that feels more like a conversation.

What All Of This Means For You

There will times that you as an IT manager will need to get your message out to your entire team. As your team has grown larger and larger, this type of communication becomes harder and harder. What you need to go is to **get good at doing some public speaking**. This is the kind of skill that most IT team building activities will require you to do.

It turns out that **it's not all that tough to deliver a great public speech**. What you need to remember to do is to tell your own story in order to remain genuine. Never speak to a nameless, faceless crowd. Take the time before the speech to mix and mingle with your audience in order to turn them into friends. Finally, keep in mind that what you want to tell your IT team is not all about you. Focus on how you can have a conversation with your team.

The good news is that by giving a speech to your team, **you can really connect with them**. It's not always easy to do this well. Use the three tips that we've discussed in order to get better at doing this. Once you've mastered the skill of public speaking, you'll have become a more powerful IT manager...

Chapter 12

In Order To Become A Better Manager, You Need To Learn How To Act Like A Girl

Chapter 12: In Order To Become A Better Manager, You Need To Learn How To Act Like A Girl

I think that we can all agree that there are **certain IT manager skills and traits that the really good managers have**. As IT managers, we'd like to discover what these traits are (is there any IT manager training for this?) and then find ways to incorporate them into our own management style. It turns out that some really smart people have been studying the people who do a good job of managing teams and what they've discovered is that we all need to become just a bit more feminine.

What Are Managers Trying To Accomplish?

Ok, I'm going to be the first one to confess that my "image" of **an effective manager** was probably shaped by the movies and TV shows that I saw when I was growing up. The managers who were able to get things done were real men: they yelled, they pounded their fists on tables, and they basically intimidated everyone into doing what they needed to have done when they needed to have it done.

Well, guess what? As with so many other things in life, **what I saw on the big screen does not really translate into real life very well**. Yes, it is possible to be the type of IT manager who does all of those manly things that we think that effective managers do, but what we'll quickly discover is that nobody wants to work on our team and those who have to are not very productive.

So what's the solution? Well, depending on how manly you are you're not going to like this very much. It turns out that the most effective managers are the ones who demonstrate traits that are traditionally considered to feminine characteristics. Sorry about this – **sensitivity is in, pounding on tables is out**.

What Qualities Should An IT Manager Have?

So should we all start wearing pastels to work and watching "Desperate Housewives" (is that even on TV anymore?) **The answer is a very clear no**. Instead, we need to identify just exactly what characteristics are going to make us a better IT managers, do away with the gender classifications, and then work them into our everyday interactions with our teams.

The big question is what traits do we need to have? It turns out that there are 7 different personality characteristics that **we all need to work at**. Here they are:

Empathy: This can be a tough one to do well. What it requires you to do is to be sensitive to the thoughts and feelings of the members of your team. This means that you need to think about what they are thinking about.

Vulnerability: In my book, this is the hardest trait of all. As an IT manager you need to acknowledge that you have limitations – you can't do it all. When you encounter a situation where you need help, you have to be willing to ask for it.

Humility: It turns out that it's not all about you. What you need to learn how to do is to find ways to serve the members of your team. When something is a success, you need to be able to share the credit with everyone who contributed.

Inclusiveness: In our fast-paced world, we like to get everything done quickly. However, in order to work better with our team, we need to learn the skills of asking for other people's options and then listening to what they have to say. This is a key part of any IT team building efforts that you conduct.

Generosity: They say that it's better to give than to receive. This means that you need to learn how to give of your advice, support, time and contacts.

Balance: You have a life and you have a job. You need to make sure that you feed both of these beasts properly.

Patience: Not everything that is important is due tomorrow. Instead, you need to teach yourself to take the long-term view of how the things that you are working on today will impact the team over the long haul.

What Does All Of This Mean For You?

Becoming a better manager is something that all of us should trying to accomplish all of the time. The difficult part of this is that it's not exactly clear **what we need to be doing in order to become better**. The good news is that experts have been studying effective managers and they tell us that what we need to do is to become more like girls.

What they mean by this is that a lot of the personality characteristics that are traditionally associated with women turn out to be **traits that leaders need to have**. These qualities include: empathy, vulnerability, humility, inclusiveness, generosity, balance, and patience.

We are entering an era where labeling traits as belonging to either men or women is started to become out-of-date. Instead, what really matters is that as IT managers we want to be equipped with the traits that will **allow us to manage our teams effectively**. It sure looks like we need to spend some time learning how to add some feminine skills to our management playbook.

It's from the forge of failure that the steel of success is formed.

Hard Work Does Not Guarantee Success, But Success Does Not Happen Without Hard Work.

- Dr. Jim Anderson

Create IT Departments That Are Productive And A Valuable Asset To The Rest Of The Company !

Dr. Jim Anderson is available to provide training and coaching on the topics that are the most important to people who have to manage IT departments: how can I build a productive IT department (and keep it together) while at the same time providing the rest of the company with the IT services that they need?

Dr. Anderson believes that in order to both learn and remember what he says, speakers need to laugh. Each one of his speeches is full of fun and humor so that what he says "sticks" with everyone.

Dr. Anderson's CIO Skills Training Includes:

1. How to identify and attract the right type of IT workers to your IT department.
2. How to build relationships with the company's senior management in order to get the support that you need?
3. How to stay on top of changing technology and security issues so that you never get surprised?

Dr. Jim Anderson works with over 100 customers per year. To invite Dr. Anderson to work with you, contact him at:

Phone: 813-418-6970 or
Email: jim@BlueElephantConsulting.com

Photo Credits:

Cover - nist6dh

https://www.flickr.com/photos/53801255@N07/

Chapter 1 - nasirkhan

https://morguefile.com/p/86729

Chapter 2 – Alvimann

https://morguefile.com/p/550793

Chapter 3 – beglib

https://morguefile.com/p/681657

Chapter 4 – anitapeppers

https://morguefile.com/p/95839

Chapter 5 – Taliesin

https://morguefile.com/p/112169

Chapter 6 - wintersixfour

https://morguefile.com/p/677219

Chapter 7 - unknown

http://www.flickr.com/photos/parl/3865066/

Chapter 8 - huggs2

https://www.flickr.com/photos/jarhue2/

Chapter 9 – Lynac

https://www.flickr.com/photos/lynac/

Chapter 10 – Rob

https://www.flickr.com/photos/gensyn/

Chapter 11 - Christian Pierret

https://www.flickr.com/photos/christianpierret/

Chapter 12 - @Doug88888

https://www.flickr.com/photos/doug88888/

Other Books By The Author

Product Management

- Manage Your Customers, Manage Your Product: Techniques For Product Managers To Better Understand What Their Customers Really Want

- How Product Managers Can Sell More Of Their Product: Tips & Techniques For Product Managers To Better Understand How To Sell Their Product

- How Product Managers Can Sell More Of Their Product: Tips & Techniques For Product Managers To Better Understand How To Sell Their Product

- How To Create A Successful Product That Customers Will Want: Techniques For Product Managers To Boost Product Sales And Increase Customer Satisfaction

- What Product Managers Need To Know About World-Class Product Development: How Product Managers Can Create Successful Products

- How Product Managers Can Learn To Understand Their Customers: Techniques For Product

Managers To Better Understand What Their
Customers Really Want

- Product Management Secrets: Techniques For
  Product Managers To Boost Product Sales And
  Increase Customer Satisfaction

- Product Development Lessons For Product
  Managers: How Product Managers Can Create
  Successful Products

- Customer Lessons For Product Managers:
  Techniques For Product Managers To Better
  Understand What Their Customers Really Want

- Product Failure Lessons For Product Managers:
  Examples Of Products That Have Failed For Product
  Managers To Learn From

- Communication Skills For Product Managers: The
  Communication Skills That Product Managers Need
  To Know How To Use In Order To Have A Successful
  Product

- How To Have A Successful Product Manager
  Career: The Things That You Need To Be Doing
  TODAY In Order To Have A Successful Product
  Manager Career

- Product Manager Product Success: How to keep your product on track and make it become a success

Public Speaking

- How To Get Ready To Give The Perfect Speech: What Tools To Use To Create Your Next Speech So That Your Message Will Be Remembered Forever!

- Creating Speeches That Work: How To Create A Speech That Will Make Your Message Be Remembered Forever!

- How To Organize A Speech In Order To Make Your Point: How to put together a speech that will capture and hold your audience's attention

- Changing How You Speak To Overcome Your Fear Of Speaking: Change techniques that will transform a speech into a memorable event

- Delivering Excellence: How To Give Presentations That Make A Difference: Presentation techniques that will transform a speech into a memorable event

- Tools Speakers Need In Order To Give The Perfect Speech: What tools to use to create your next speech so that your message will be remembered forever!

- How To Create A Speech That Will Be Remembered

- Secrets To Organizing A Speech For Maximum Impact: How to put together a speech that will capture and hold your audience's attention

- How To Become A Better Speaker By Changing How You Speak: Change techniques that will transform a speech into a memorable event

- How To Give A Great Presentation: Presentation techniques that will transform a speech into a memorable event

- How To Rehearse In Order To Give The Perfect Speech: How to effectively rehearse your next speech to that your message be remembered forever!

- Secrets To Creating The Perfect Speech: How to create a speech that will make your message be remembered forever!

- Secrets To Organizing The Perfect Speech: How to organize the best speech of your life!

- Secrets To Planning The Perfect Speech: How to plan to give the best speech of your life

- How To Show What You Mean During A Presentation: How to use visual techniques to transform a speech into a memorable event

CIO Skills

- How CIOs Can Take Their Career To The Next Level: How CIOs Can Work With The Entire Company In Order To Be Successful

- How CIOs Can Bring Business And IT Together: How CIOs Can Use Their Technical Skills To Help Their Company Solve Real-World Business Problems

- New IT Technology Issues Facing CIOs: How CIOs Can Stay On Top Of The Changes In The Technology That Powers The Company

- Keeping The Barbarians Out: How CIOs Can Secure Their Department and Company: Tips And Techniques For CIOs To Use In Order To Secure Both Their IT Department And Their Company

- What CIOs Need To Know In Order To Successfully Manage An IT Department: Decision Making Skills That Every CIO Needs To Have In Order To Be Able

To Make The Right Choices

- Becoming A Powerful And Effective Leader: Tips And Techniques That IT Managers Can Use In Order To Develop Leadership Skills

- CIO Secrets For Growing Innovation: Tips And Techniques For CIOs To Use In Order To Make Innovation Happen In Their IT Department

- Your Success As A CIO Depends On How Well You Communicate: Tips And Techniques For CIOs To Use In Order To Become Better Communicators

- What CIOs Need To Know About Working With Partners: Techniques For CIOs To Use In Order To Be Able To Successfully Work With Partners

- Critical CIO Management Skills: Decision Making Skills That Every CIO Needs To Have In Order To Be Able To Make The Right Choices

- How CIOs Can Make Innovation Happen: Tips And Techniques For CIOs To Use In Order To Make Innovation Happen In Their IT Department

- CIO Communication Skills Secrets: Tips And Techniques For CIOs To Use In Order To Become

Better Communicators

- Managing Your CIO Career: Steps That CIOs Have To Take In Order To Have A Long And Successful Career

- CIO Business Skills: How CIOs can work effectively with the rest of the company!

IT Manager Skills

- How IT Managers Can Use New Technology To Meet Today's IT Challenges: Technologies That IT Managers Can Use In Order to Make Their Teams More Productive

- How To Build High Performance IT Teams: Tips And Techniques That IT Managers Can Use In Order To Develop Productive Teams

- Save Yourself, Save Your Job – How To Manage Your IT Career: Secrets That IT Managers Can Use In Order To Have A Successful Career

- Growing Your CIO Career: How CIOs Can Work With The Entire Company In Order To Be Successful

- How IT Managers Can Make Innovation Happen: Tips And Techniques For IT Managers To Use In

Order To Make Innovation Happen In Their Teams

- Staffing Skills IT Managers Must Have: Tips And Techniques That IT Managers Can Use In Order To Correctly Staff Their Teams

- Secrets Of Effective Leadership For IT Managers: Tips And Techniques That IT Managers Can Use In Order To Develop Leadership Skills

- IT Manager Career Secrets: Tips And Techniques That IT Managers Can Use In Order To Have A Successful Career

- IT Manager Budgeting Skills: How IT Managers Can Request, Manage, Use, And Track Their Funding

- Secrets Of Managing Budgets: What IT Managers Need To Know In Order To Understand How Their Company Uses Money

Negotiating

- The Art Of Packaging A Negotiation: How To Develop The Skill Of Assembling Potential Trades In Order To Get The Best Possible Outcome

- Getting What You Want In A Negotiation By Learning How To Signal: How To Develop The Skill Of Effective

Signaling In A Negotiation In Order To Get The Best Possible Outcome

- Exploring How To Get The Deal That You Want In A Negotiation: How To Develop The Skill Of Exploring What Is Possible In A Negotiation In Order To Reach The Best Possible Deal

- Use The Power Of Arguing To Win Your Next Negotiation: How To Develop The Skill Of Effective Arguing In A Negotiation In Order To Get The Best Possible Outcome

- Learn How To Signal In Your Next Negotiation: How To Develop The Skill Of Effective Signaling In A Negotiation In Order To Get The Best Possible Outcome

- Learn The Skill Of Exploring In A Negotiation: How To Develop The Skill Of Exploring What Is Possible In A Negotiation In Order To Reach The Best Possible Deal

- Learn How To Argue In Your Next Negotiation: How To Develop The Skill Of Effective Arguing In A Negotiation In Order To Get The Best Possible Outcome|

- How To Open Your Next Negotiation: How To Start A Negotiation In Order To Get The Best Possible Outcome

- Preparing For Your Next Negotiation: What You Need To Do BEFORE A Negotiation Starts In Order To Get The Best Possible Deal

- Learn How To Package Trades In Your Next Negotiation

- All Good Things Come To An End: How To Close A Negotiation - How To Develop The Skill Of Closing In Order To Get The Best Possible Outcome From A Negotiation

- Take No Prisoners In Your Next Negotiation: How To Start A Negotiation In Order To Get The Best Possible Outcome

Miscellaneous

- How To Heal A Broken Leg – Fast!: Understanding how to deal with a broken leg in order to start walking again quickly

- How Software Defined Networking (SDN) Is Going To Change Your World Forever: The Revolution In

Network Design And How It Affects You

- The Power Of Virtualization: How It Affects Memory, Servers, and Storage: The Revolution In Creating Virtual Devices And How It Affects You

- The Internet-Enabled Successful School District Superintendent: How To Use The Internet To Boost Parental Involvement In Your Schools

- Power Distribution Unit (PDU) Secrets: What Everyone Who Works In A Data Center Needs To Know!

- Making The Jump: How To Land Your Dream Job When You Get Out Of College!

- How To Use The Internet To Create Successful Students And Involved Parents

"Tips And Techniques That IT Managers Can Use In Order To Develop Leadership Skills"

> This book has been written with one goal in mind – to show you how an IT manager can build needed leadership skills. It's not easy being an IT manager so we're going to show you what you need to be doing in order to not only manage your team, but to also be a leader to them!
>
> **Let's Make Your IT Career A Success!**

<u>What You'll Find Inside:</u>

- **YOU CAN BE AN IT LEADER, HERE'S HOW...**

- **IT MANAGER LEADERSHIP: TWO WAYS TO LEAD WHEN YOU'RE NOT IN CHARGE**

- **5 THINGS THAT AN IT MANAGER NEEDS TO KNOW ABOUT RISK**

- **HOW AN IT LEADER CAN MOTIVATE THEIR TEAM**

Dr. Jim Anderson brings his 25 years of real-world experience to this book. He's been an IT manager at some of the world's largest firms. He's going to show you what you need to do (and not do!) in order to successfully manage your career!

www.ingramcontent.com/pod-product-compliance
Lightning Source LLC
Chambersburg PA
CBHW071758170526
45167CB00003B/1083